THE PHILOSOPHY OF
WHISKY

THE PHILOSOPHY OF
WHISKY

BILLY ABBOTT

First published 2021 by
The British Library
96 Euston Road
London NW1 2DB

ISBN 978 0 7123 5455 4
eISBN 978 0 7123 6704 2
Cataloguing in Publication Data
A catalogue record for this book is available
from the British Library

Designed and typeset by Sandra Friesen
Printed in Malta by Gutenberg Press

CONTENTS

WHAT IS WHISKY?

[Whisky] is a toast to civilization, a tribute to the continuity of culture, a manifesto of man's determination to use the resources of nature to refresh mind and body and enjoy to the full the senses with which he has been endowed.

— David Daiches, *Scotch Whisky*

THE HUMAN RACE is quite clever. Over the millennia we have managed to develop language, invent the wheel, create incredible works of art, survive global crises and even fling ourselves beyond our tiny blue dot into the heavens. But alongside these big hitters there stands another achievement: one that continues to develop, intertwined with – and, in many cases, closely connected to – how we got to where we are today. I speak, of course, of the creation of whisky.

Whisky is built upon the very foundations of society, and has both drawn from and contributed to everything from agriculture to the most recent advances in technology.

Whisky has, since its beginnings, been at the heart of everything.

Which isn't bad for a batch of dodgy porridge that someone boiled up, left in a bucket and forgot about.

To start with, what is whisky? It's a question I've given much consideration to over the years – and when you move away from the metaphysical, it comes down to a succession of poor versions of other things, which finally come good when you stop messing about with them.

STEP 1: Make some bad porridge. Now, many people around the globe – and I'm mostly looking at you, Scotland – will disagree, but I don't really consider smashed-up grains mixed with water a particularly tasty breakfast. I want milk. And sugar. Or potentially cheese. But whisky starts from that meagre gruel: milled grain and water.

STEP 2: Use your porridge to make some bad beer. Not only that, but a low-tech beer that most of the world moved on from years ago. Most distillers' beer (aka 'wash') smells a bit like a cloudy Belgian wheat beer, but without much of the nuance those beers often have or the pleasant experience that drinking one can provide. It's cloudy, full of yeast, grain and other gunk, and a few sips can lead to a 'catastrophic gastrointestinal event' – not a beverage to enjoy with your friends of an evening.

STEP 3: Distil your beer to make bad vodka. Vodka is a spirit often associated with purity, carefully distilled to remove almost all flavour. When you make whisky, you want the opposite: a stinky, strong-tasting drink that you need to leave for a while to make it palatable.

STEP 4: Stick your 'vodka' in a cask and forget about it. While whisky takes different amounts of time to mature around the world, this step is key to creating something that is distinctly 'whisky' rather than an unaged firewater. Time sitting in wood creates and develops the flavours that make whisky into whisky, and it can take decades to make the spirit the distiller wants. So, fill a barrel, put it in the corner and forget about it – but when you remember it's there, you'll thank me.

It is a near-universal rule that if there is a source of sugar, then someone is making an alcoholic drink from it. Be it my school friends trying to brew 'wine' in a Marmite jar hidden under their beds,[1] or the centuries-old wine-making families of France, it's clear that if there is something that contains sugar in almost any form, it can and will be turned into alcohol.

With grain it's not so easy, as its sugar is wrapped up in a form that is not simple to turn into booze. But people are clever, and as we developed the foundations of agriculture, so too did we learn how to trick grains into giving up their sweetness, leading to the creation of beer.

We didn't stop there. While distillation may have begun as a way of concentrating flavours to create perfume, it

---

1 I made a tidy income while at school supplying bread yeast to friends who didn't want to be seen buying their own in the local supermarket, wary that a scarily insightful adult would guess their intentions. Rather than creating fine wines and beers, this generally turned cheap fruit juice into a rotten, undrinkable mess that they would claim was 'as strong as vodka'. I never got into illicit brewing, instead spending my ill-gotten gains on going to the pub, where I would drink beer that was much cheaper and less prone to causing violent illness.

wasn't that long before we realised you could use it to not only make your beer last longer, but also produce a drink that made you fall over even faster. Science and engineering principles are often driven from theory into practice by our baser instincts, and our love of drink has certainly helped push agriculture, microbiology and chemical engineering into the future.

The knowledge of whisky making has since travelled around the world. Whether it was missionaries importing religion with a side order of booze, or settlers finding new lands and looking for something to sip in the evening while they fought off wolves, wherever people have gone, whisky has soon followed.

5

In the end, whisky really is a drink that taps into what it means to be human. It's been with us since we first combined science and food, has spread around the world as we have become a global species, and has prevailed as a drink of the people as we have matured. It's a drink with a long history that goes right to the heart of the societies it sprang from, and a glass of whisky today has roots that extend to every part of the world.

And it tastes nice.

WHISKY OR WHISKEY?

Whisky is a social drink and, as any attendee of a social gathering can attest, when you mix alcohol and people, there will be an argument.

One of the most common disagreements in the whisky world is how to spell the word itself. Over the years, two spellings have emerged: whisky and whiskey. While they were both in common use back in the nineteenth century, an era where the spelling of the English language was still in the process of being standardised, these days things are a bit more defined. While there are many debates, things are actually quite simple:

☞ WHISKEY – most (but not all) American and Irish whiskey.
☞ WHISKY – whisky made everywhere else in the world.

Throughout the book I will use the most relevant spelling, depending on context.

However, if you find yourself arguing over how to spell the word, I'd advise that you take a step back, have a long hard think about what you're doing and then pour another glass of whisk(e)y.

THE INGREDIENTS

WHISKY IS, in essence, a simple drink: make some very old-fashioned beer, boil it up, collect the steam and then put it in something wooden. While for many years the final step was optional, the past century has seen whisky become a cornerstone of the world of 'brown spirits', sitting alongside brandy at the top of the pile.

Its simple ingredients belie the potential differences down the line. No matter how many different styles, types and brands of whisky we might find in bottles, they all start from the same simple ingredients: grain, yeast, wood and time.

GRAIN

If you can look into the seeds of time,
And say which grain will grow and which will not,
Speak then to me, who neither beg nor fear
Your favours, nor your hate.

— William Shakespeare, *Macbeth*

Grains are, fittingly, seeds. Not only can one grow a plant from a grain, but it is also the source of all of whisky – without grains, we would have none.

Around the world, a huge range of different grains are used. While you can find buckwheat, rice and triticale spirit, in the end most is made from the big four: barley, maize, rye and wheat.

Barley is ancient, having been cultivated for as long as 10,000 years; it was one of the first domesticated crops. It can grow in most of the inhabited parts of the world and, as such, is one of the most popular grains. Over the years, it has become less common as a human food, and generally has a pair of main uses: feeding animals and making booze.

Barley beer was one of the first alcoholic drinks to be developed, reliably appearing in the historical record by 5,000 BC. In the following millennia it spread throughout the world and is now the third most popular drink, beaten only by tea and water. Unsurprisingly, it is at the heart of the earliest spirits that led us to modern whisky.

Wheat is a grain that has been used by humans for as long as barley but, unlike barley, it is still a staple food – there is more land dedicated to growing wheat in the world than any other crop, and it is only beaten by maize in tonnage produced. It is the default choice for making bread, and as such is eaten by most of the world's population on a daily basis. In the drinks world, wheat is much less commonly used than barley – a side effect of it being a popular food – but it is a key component in many whisky traditions.

Rye is a versatile grain, albeit a comparative newcomer in the world of domesticated crops. Well known in Eurasia, it travelled to the Americas and became a popular crop there, forming the basis of the early whiskeys made by European settlers.

Maize – aka corn – is the grain that has been used by humans the longest, with evidence pointing to its domestication in Mexico more than 10,000 years ago. It is now the most cultivated crop in the world, but it only made it into drinks comparatively recently. While there are traditions of maize beer in South America, distillation came with European settlers, and corn spirits followed not far behind.

These four grains – whether used alone or in combination – give most whisky its starting point. They create the

MALTING

Despite being commonly used to make alcoholic drinks, grains need a bit of work before they are ready to be used to make booze.

Grains are seeds, and are packed with sugars that the growing plant will use to give it energy. However, in their raw, straight-off-the-plant form, the sugars in grains are tied up in such a way that we cannot easily turn them into alcohol. They are coiled up in starch, long chains of sugar molecules that we must break down before we can do this.

The standard process used to do this is malting. In essence, malting is tricking a plant to start growing. You get the grain wet, then dry it out, then get it wet again, then dry it out again, and so on. After a while the grain, experiencing the conditions it might in a field, will start releasing enzymes that will help break down the long starch chains. At this point, before too much of the starch is broken down, the grain is dried out, halting the process. The resulting grain is called malt, and it is now ready to be turned, eventually, into whisky.

flavours and chemical precursors that the rest of the whisky-making process will build on to create the final spirit.

YEAST

Fermentation may have been a greater discovery than fire.

— David Rains Wallace

When it comes to whisky making, yeast doesn't get much attention. Speak to most whisky fans and they'll wax lyrical about grain and wood, but rarely will they dive into the microbiological world of yeast and fermentation. Unfortunately, fungi aren't usually considered sexy, even though they are hugely important when making whisky – without yeast, not only do we not have the flavour of whisky, but we don't have any alcohol.

Yeast is everywhere. There are more than 1,000 species and we are quite literally surrounded by them. You are almost certainly covered in yeast, as is this book, and pretty much everything else around you. However, most yeasts aren't very useful to whisky makers – we need yeast that can turn sugar into alcohol without making things taste horrible.

The most common species used is *Saccharomyces cerevisiae*, and it pops up across the worlds of bread and drinks. Feed the yeast some sugar and it'll produce carbon dioxide, alcohol and flavour – a process known as fermentation, which makes bread rise, creates booze and bubbles in beer and gives both loads of flavour. The apples and pears of Scotch whisky, the bananas of Jack Daniel's and the mango and pineapple of Asian whiskies all come from yeast. Next time you're enjoying a fruity whisky, make sure to raise a toast to friendly fungi everywhere.

WOOD

Whisky matures in the cask and not in the bottle, and the kind of cask in which it matures is, of course, important.

— David Daiches, *Scotch Whisky*

We will never know which inventive distiller first decided to store their spirit in a cask, but whoever it was may be the true creator of whisky, whether they lived in Scotland, Ireland or even Egypt. However, while storing freshly distilled spirits in ceramic or glass – containers that themselves don't add flavour – can help the spirits to soften and develop over time, it is wood that really defines whisky.

There are many numbers bandied around when it comes to precisely how much flavour a whisky gets from its casks, but for me there's only one that makes sense – 100 per cent: by which I mean that all the whisky in a cask is affected by the wood to some extent. Exactly how much flavour that will be will vary from cask to cask and depends

on a huge range of factors, from the make-up of the spirit, temperature, air pressure and humidity to the history of the cask itself.

When it comes to making casks for whisky, we tend to focus on oak. Oak, like grain, is found the world over. And, also like grain, every country has its own. From the tall and straight trunks of North America to the twisted and gnarly branches of Spanish oak, not only do the trees look different, but their woods are different in their handling, and the flavours they impart to spirits vary wildly.

While it's not the only wood used to make casks, oak is the most common when it comes to making whisky. It's easily worked and doesn't leak as much as other types of wood – chestnut might give some interesting flavours, but if the whisky ends up on the floor of your warehouse, it doesn't really matter. It's not only the type of wood that makes a difference, though, but how the cask has been used.

The first time a cask is filled, it will have lots to give – oak is rich with flavour, but each time you refill it there will be less left. But every time a cask is used, an imprint of its occupant will remain. This dual imprint, with flavour being both removed from the wood and left behind, means a cask of new oak filled for the first time will give very different flavours and character compared to a cask that was once filled with sherry and has been used to mature whisky since.

It's these choices combined with one final ingredient that will create our whisky.

TIME

Whisky is 'slow'. It speaks of place, craftmanship and a timeless approach to taking an ingredient and magically extracting its essence.

— Dave Broom, *The World Atlas of Whisky*

It might seem strange to include time as an ingredient but, abstract though it is, time is key. When spirit comes off the still, it is not usually ready to be drunk. It needs to settle, rest and develop – time is of the essence.

Time does many things to a spirit, especially one stored in wood. Chemical reactions aren't instantaneous, and the development of flavour both within the spirit and through interaction with the cask needs time. While lots of flavour comes from the wood, the spirit itself is packed with character, and time does not leave it alone. The spirit is a roiling mess at first, and slow reactions will create new flavours as well as slowly amplifying and transforming those already there. Throw in the flavours added by the wood, and you have even more to play with, and the interactions of all of these will create complexity over time.

That's not to say that adding time will make things better. A brand-new cask of spirit left for a long time may become too woody, the oak overwhelming the flavour of the grain and fermentation. A delicate spirit in a many-times-used cask will probably need much longer not only to extract flavour from the wood, but also to evolve and develop complexity. Time is just one more ingredient, and it must be balanced against everything else.

Making whisky is much more an art than a science. With so many variables involved, the result can be chaotic and difficult to predict. The experience of the whisky makers, handed down through generations, coupled with skilful manipulation of ingredients and process, all pushes the whisky to its final, tasty destination.

WHISKY AROUND
THE WORLD

*How solemn and beautiful is the thought that the earliest
pioneer of civilization, the van-leader of civilization,
is never the steamboat, never the railroad, never the
newspaper, never the sabbath school, never the missionary
– but always whisky!*

— Mark Twain, *Life on the Mississippi*

BACK IN THE mists of time, there was *uisge/uisce beatha*
– Scottish and Irish Gaelic for 'the water of life'. While
the name has developed over time, the spirit itself has also
changed beyond recognition. Made from leftover grain,
these early proto-whiskies were more akin to gin – unaged
spirits flavoured with fruit, herbs and honey. Initially they
would have been a way to use up grain that might otherwise
have gone bad, but wherever they have been made, they
have soon become a staple.

In the centuries since it first appeared, we have seen
whisky change, develop and spread around the world.

When you look at a modern whisky, its history is woven tightly into its DNA: a history of the people who made it, and of farming, trade and technology. Only in understanding its origin can we truly understand a whisky.

SCOTLAND

The whisky of this country is a most rascally liquor;
and by consequence only drank by the most rascally part
of the inhabitants.

— Robert Burns, Letter to Mr John Tennant,
22 December 1788

WHEN PEOPLE TALK about whisky without saying anything
about where it's from, they're usually talking about spirit
from Scotland – Scotch whisky. This, more than any other
country's whisky, has become an icon of the spirit world,
and it has been so for a surprisingly long time. Its early
history is a blueprint for whisky around the world, and its
development into the spirit it is today has informed – for
both good and ill – whisky makers everywhere.

Like so many other spirits, it started out as a rough and
rustic farmhouse spirit, the result of needing to turn grain
into something that wouldn't go mouldy quite as easily.
The grain most commonly associated with Scotch whisky

is barley – the same today as it was when set down in the first written record of any Scottish spirit in 1494.

The beginning of modern Scottish whisky making arrived in 1655 with the first government interference – the imposition of taxes. No longer was spirit all home-distilled, where it was notoriously hard to justify taxes. Instead, we start to see commercial whisky making.

By this time, whisky was more as we know it now – distilled from malted barley and matured in wooden casks to give it the colour and the distinctive flavour it is known for. Distillers had moved on from the days of unaged, herb-dosed spirits and firmly into making something we would recognise.

IRELAND OR SCOTLAND: WHO MADE WHISK(E)Y FIRST?

The longest-running debate in the whisky world is who made it first. Scotland and Ireland are traditionally pointed to as the originators, and when it comes to the modern(ish) written record, we have a pair of entries.

IRELAND: The *Annals of Clonmacnoise* – '1405. Richard or Risdard maGrannell, chieftaine of Moyntireolas, died at Christmas by takeing a surfeit of aqua vitae, to him aqua mortis.'

SCOTLAND: The Exchequer Rolls of 1 June 1494 – 'And by allowance made to Brother John Cor by precept of the comptroller, as he asserts, by the King's command, to make aquavite within the period of the account, eight bolls of malt.'

Both suggest that *aqua vitae* – Latin for 'water of life' – was around a while before the records were written, so choosing a winner is difficult. All we can safely say is that both countries have been distilling for a long time.

I find the easiest way to get people from Ireland and Scotland to come to an agreement on the subject is to suggest that the English invented whisky – the resounding 'no' this statement elicits is about as close as we'll get.

The first documented distillery was Ferintosh, and that initial mention is of its destruction in 1689. It would have entirely faded into history, as its contemporaries mostly have, had it not been immortalised the following year by Robert Burns – the bard of Scotland – in his poem 'Scotch Drink':

Thee, Ferintosh! Oh, sadly lost!
Scotland lament frae coast to coast!

While larger distilleries were easier for the Crown to tax, smaller operations and household stills were notoriously difficult to uncover, leading to a culture of illicit distillation. Scotland is a land of hills and valleys, and hiding a still from government officials – the excisemen, known as gaugers – was much easier then than it would be today. A culture of distrust of authority, a love of distilled spirit and a network of locals ready to pass on information when a gauger was spotted all helped to keep the distillers going. The ability to break down a still and hide it before the excisemen found you became a key skill.

Distillers and smugglers fought a quiet war with the excisemen for decades, with the situation occasionally escalating into violence. Reforms imposed greater taxes on the distillers of Scotland over the years, leading to more and more illicit spirit being produced and smuggled. While the penalties for breaking the law were harsh, the rewards were great, and the prevalence and fame of the illicit spirit grew.

The situation came to a head with George IV's state visit to Scotland in 1822. Accompanied by Sir Walter Scott and with his head filled with romantic stories of clans, tartan and tradition, the king toured the country, greeted by pageantry and celebrations that were often created especially for the visit rather than having any basis in history. During the trip, it is said that he called for whisky and, rather than anything legal, asked for 'the real Glenlivet'. This is not to be confused with the Glenlivet distillery that enjoys worldwide fame today, but instead referred to whisky from the Glen Livet, the valley through which the River Livet flows. It is now known as the heart of Speyside, the region

of Scotland most densely packed with distilleries, but at the time it was a haven for illicit stills, with more than 200 distillers producing spirit there.

'Real Glenlivet' wasn't a distillery, but instead an allusion to 'real whisky' – the spirit drunk by the Scots of Sir Walter's tales, and if it was good enough for the king … Whisky's popularity continued to grow after George's visit, spreading beyond Scotland's borders.

While the stories around the king's visit are almost certainly as romanticised as the pomp and ceremony he saw on his tour, it was a time of change in Scottish whisky making. More distillers decided to become legal, paying their taxes and creating the names we still know today. The years leading up to the king's trip saw many distilleries establish themselves with licences and move out of the shadows of illicit distillation.

The commercial world was very different back in the nineteenth century, and distilleries dealt primarily in casks of whisky rather than bottles. Casks would be sold to grocers and great houses with cellars full of drinks, who would then serve it up by the bottle or glass as appropriate.

Over the years, the grocers and whisky merchants grew to become the backbone of the whisky trade, the conduit through which the public obtained and drank whisky. While it was possible to buy 'self whisky' – whisky from a single distillery – the merchants also made blends of malt whisky, creating their own ongoing mixtures either by design or necessity, smoothing out supply as casks from one distiller dried up and were replaced by others. It was in this era that a new invention changed the path of whisky history, especially in Scotland: the patenting of the Coffey still.

It was named after inventor – and former exciseman – Aeneas Coffey. His patented still created a new type of spirit, which we now called grain whisky. His still differed from more traditional stills by not only being able to distil to a much higher alcoholic strength, but also by being able to run continuously, rather than having to stop and start repeatedly. Theoretically, as long as you fed in your beer to be distilled, there would be a flow of spirit out, making

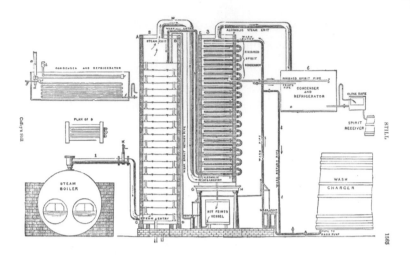

it significantly more efficient and cheaper to run than old-fashioned stills.

The spirit these stills produced was lighter and less intensely flavoured than malt spirit, but the grocers combined it with traditional, richly flavoured malt whisky to create a style that slowly rose in popularity. The three styles of whisky of the time – self whisky, blends of malts and blends of grain and malt – are still the backbone of the Scottish whisky world today, enshrined in law as single malt, blended malt and blended whisky: malt whisky from one distillery, a blend of malt whiskies from different distilleries and a blend of malt and grain whisky.

At the time, brandy was the king of spirits, and a major reason for the rising popularity of Scotch whisky was French brandy's almost-disappearance. In the mid-nineteenth

TRADE MARK AND LABEL OF MESSRS GRANT OF GLEN-GRANT.

century, a strange blight started affecting grape vines in the South of France – the first documented occurrence of what became known as the Great French Wine Blight. Behind the scenes, it was all down to an insect – an aphid which came to be known as 'grape phylloxera' – imported from the Americas, which fed on the vines and damaged their roots. By the 1870s, it had caused the destruction of as much as 40 per cent of France's vineyards.

While the wine industry was eventually saved thanks to phylloxera-resistant plants from the US, there was a significant dip in the production of wine and, as a consequence, brandy – distilled wine. A milder and more delicate drink than a traditional Scottish whisky, brandy was the choice of the aristocracy, and an aspirational drink for everyone else. With a gap in supply of their drink of choice, brandy drinkers looked to alternatives and found blended Scotch whisky – a lighter and more delicate take on the traditional malt. This, combined with changing palates, the rise of marketing and mass communication, and changes in the way that people bought drinks, all led to blended whisky pulling ahead of its counterparts and becoming the most popular style of Scotch whisky.

The grocers behind these early blends are names that are still well known to us today: John Walker, Arthur Bell, William Teacher, John Dewar, brothers John and James Chivas, and James Whyte and Charles Mackay. They created the first true Scotch whisky brands and took them to

Born 1820
—*Still going strong.*

Stranger, arriving at a Scotch country station : "WHICH HOTEL DO YOU RECOMMEND ?"
Porter : "THERE'S ONLY WAN."
Stranger : "WHY, I THOUGHT THERE WERE TWO ! "
Porter : "THERE'S ONLY WAN AS KEEPS 'JOHNNIE WALKER,' SO THE ITHER DISNA COONT."

It is a safe rule to follow, that an hotel which discriminates as to the quality of its whisky will always give satisfaction.

Every drop of "Johnnie Walker" Black Label is over 12 years old.

GUARANTEED SAME QUALITY THROUGHOUT THE WORLD.

JOHN WALKER & SONS, LTD., SCOTCH WHISKY DISTILLERS, KILMARNOCK.

the world. From Whyte & Mackay and Johnnie Walker's initial forays into the Australian market in the early twentieth century to Chivas Regal's creation for the American market, the Scottish blenders established their names and quickly took them to all corners of the earth. Even now, the vast majority of Scotch whisky drunk around the world is a blend of malt and grain – blended whisky today makes up as much as 90 per cent of the world whisky market.

However, that figure was much higher in past decades. The wheel has turned, and what was old is new again: single malts are on the rise. Since the middle of the twentieth century, both whisky merchants and the distillers themselves – often now the same companies after decades of consolidation – have focused more on single malts as they have grown in popularity. The years since have seen single malts make their way to the top of the pile, with a growing reputation placing them above blends and allowing them slowly to take their place as the pinnacle of not only Scotch whisky, but also the wider whisky world.

SINGLE MALT, GRAIN AND BLENDS

S cotland has a robust legal framework for describing whisky, and the terminology has been adopted by many other countries around the world.

There are five types of whisky made in Scotland, and the words to describe them break down into two groups.

First, we have malt and grain. Malt whisky uses solely malted barley in its grain recipe and is distilled in traditional copper pot stills. Grain whisky is anything that doesn't meet that standard. In practice, it will almost always be made using wheat or corn and distilled in modern continuous stills.

Then there are single and blended whiskies. The former means that the whisky in your bottle was made at one distillery; the latter that the whisky is a mixture of whiskies from more than one distillery or more than one type.

Combining these two terms gives us our styles of whisky:

SINGLE MALT WHISKY – malt whisky from one distillery.
SINGLE GRAIN WHISKY – grain whisky from one distillery.
BLENDED MALT WHISKY – a mixture of malt whiskies from different distilleries.
BLENDED GRAIN WHISKY – a mixture of grain whiskies from different distilleries.

And, just to round things out, we have one more style: blended whisky, the most popular one – a mixture of malt and grain whisky.

IRELAND

The light music of whiskey falling into a glass — an agreeable interlude.

— James Joyce

IRISH WHISKEY'S STORY is not only both similar to and very different from Scotland's at various times, but is also frequently intertwined with it. The movement of people between the Celtic nations makes the point of where whisk(e)y originated fairly moot, but it's safe to say that they've been making spirits in Ireland for a very long time.

While the mention of *aqua vitae* in the *Annals of Clonmacnoise* may predate the Scottish Exchequer Rolls (see page 23), the spirit back then was probably not whiskey as we know it today. Scottish spirit was grain based, but the Irish might have started with a slightly more highbrow drink – brandy, made from imported wine. Whatever the spirit was made from, the knowledge of distillation started with the church, in the monasteries across Europe that functioned as libraries of knowledge. It soon spread to farmers and Irish distilling tradition began to grow.

The first written record of an Irish grain spirit is found in 1556. The weak English-run government passed a law to direct wheat to bread-making rather than booze production. The new law described *aqua vitae* as '... a drink nothing profitable to be daily drunken and used is now universally available through this realm, especially in the borders of the Irishry, whereby much corn, grain, and other things, are consumed.' *Aqua vitae* had now crossed over into the world of grain and was being made in such quantities that food supplies were being threatened.

By the time James VI of Scotland became King of England and Ireland in 1603, England's hold on Ireland had grown enough for it to start trying to control local industry, and he granted monopolies to local lords and institutions. These monopolies only applied to commercial distillation, and farmers continued to make spirit from leftover grain. This spirit was still at a similar stage to Scottish whisky – dosed with fruit, herbs and honey – and more similar to gin than the whiskey we know today. However, the quality of the spirit grew, and with that its reputation.

The next big change came in 1662 when English spirit taxes reached Ireland, forcing much of the home distillation underground. While distillers in the countryside could hide their stills from the taxman, urban distillers were more easily discovered. In order to cover the taxes they had to pay, they needed to operate as more commercial operations, leading to a continued trend for the growth of larger distilleries in cities.

By 1779, commercial distillation was big business and taxation was changed to focus on the size of the still rather than what was produced. This led to smaller producers having either to stop or go underground, and encouraged larger producers to run their stills more often, producing greater quantities of often low-quality spirit. The number of distillers dropped again, with production being focused on a few in the big Irish cities.

Malt taxes also made their way across the Irish Sea. This made malted barley – now the mainstay of Celtic distillation – prohibitively expensive, and the distillers looked to cheaper alternatives. While Irish whiskey had always used a variety of raw materials, this is the point at which the country's own style of whiskey emerges, the confusingly named 'pot still', made to this day using a mixture of grains – especially unmalted barley, wheat and oats, all of which avoided the malt tax.

In 1801, the Act(s) of Union created the United Kingdom of Great Britain and Ireland, and taxes continued to rise. With the newly united country engaged in overseas wars with the French and then America, the government needed money. Peace didn't help, with the Corn Laws appearing and putting high prices on imported grain, driving up the prices of local produce.

Distilleries were hard pushed to keep up and in 1823, with the Irish whiskey industry under threat of collapsing, the government helped out with the Distilleries Bill. This eased the tax burden, making things easier for whiskey makers, and leading to an explosion of new distilleries in the towns of Ireland. With barriers to entry lowered prices dropped, and Ireland's first whiskey boom began.

It was not to be plain sailing. While the church had been the cradle of Irish distillation, it also became one of its biggest opponents. On 10 April 1838, the Reverend Theobald Mathew – Father Mathew to his followers – founded the Total Abstinence Society, which later became known as the Knights of Father Mathew. Members pledged to refrain from the consumption of intoxicating liquors, and over the following decade more than 3 million people signed up, almost half of Ireland's population.

Shortly after, Ireland's food supply, already on shaky ground due to the high prices caused by the Corn Laws, was hit by potato blight, leading to mass hunger across the country. The Great Famine lasted from 1845 until the 1850s and led to more than a million deaths from hunger, and another million people leaving Ireland to escape the hardship. Wheat and oats were needed for food, leaving barley increasingly as the dominant grain in whiskey making. With Ireland's population decreasing, the local market for whiskey contracted, and the distillers looked further afield to sell their wares. Fortunately, Irish whiskey already had a

STILL HOUSE, FROM ONE OF THE GALLERIES.

following overseas – with unsold whiskey sat in warehouses and North America hungry for imported goods, Irish spirit commanded a premium and continued to develop beyond its more rough and ready origins. By the 1870s it was outselling Scotch whisky by as much as double in some markets, and had become the most popular whiskey in the world.

With success came the seeds of downfall, and as the market grew, so did the amount of lower-quality spirit available, with makers hoping to cash in on Irish whiskey's reputation. Spirit from overseas was imported and either blended with or relabelled as Irish whiskey, and a range of additives from boot polish to sulphuric acid found their way into the whiskey to stretch it further more cheaply.

Alongside these more nefarious practices was the biggest innovation in whiskey making in centuries – the rise of the column still. While Aeneas Coffey's invention had been mostly ignored in Ireland when it appeared in the 1830s – grain was expensive, and the Irish distillers' focus was on barley-based pot still whiskey – its embracing in Scotland and the rise of blended Scotch whisky's popularity led to Coffey stills appearing in Dublin, and the blending of local malt and grain. Irish blends grew in popularity, despite the opposition of the more traditional distillers, and the repeal of the Corn Laws led to an influx of cheap American maize, perfect for making grain spirit.

The scale of production at the time was huge. In the 1870s, Dublin's four biggest distillers – John Jameson at Bow Street, Powers at John's Lane, William Jameson at Marrowbone Lane and George Roe's at Thomas Street – were producing more than 20 million litres of spirit a year, similar to Scotland's largest distilleries today. However, the big four focused on more traditional distilling, and fought against the adulteration of Irish whiskey and the continued advance of blends.

It's in this era where we start seeing more consistent use of an 'e' in whiskey. While whisky and whiskey had both been used over the years, the Cork distillers started using the 'e' to distinguish themselves from the Dublin distillers – it was a sign of quality, as Dublin whiskey's reputation wobbled. Over the years, the use of the 'e' spread

as producers tried to associate themselves with the Cork distillers, and it quickly became the regular spelling.

Despite the reputational issues, Irish whiskey was still booming, with bottles exported around the world and even outselling locally made whisky in Scotland. This was very much the end of the road, though, and the coming decades saw a steep fall from grace.

The First World War halted production, as grain and spirit were redirected to the war effort. In the aftermath of the war, calls for Irish independence came to a head, and the Easter Rising led to the Irish War of Independence. With the country fighting, whiskey making fell by the wayside, and Scotland jumped on the opportunity. By the time of the foundation of the Irish Free State and the end of the Irish Civil War in 1923, the world had changed. The US, previously a huge export market for Irish whiskey, had started Prohibition and blocked all legal imports of alcohol. Instead, counterfeit Irish whiskey sloshed around in the US and tarnished the spirit's reputation to such an extent that when Prohibition was repealed, it was no longer welcome on the nation's shelves.

The 1930s also saw the Anglo-Irish Economic War and the Great Depression, effectively shutting down export. After decades of war and famine, the Irish domestic market couldn't sustain the local distillers, and closures were frequent. As trade started to stabilise in the late 1930s, the Second World War broke out, killing any hope of a recovery.

Distilleries continued to close and, in 1966, three of the largest remaining companies – Jameson, Powers and Cork Distillers – merged in an attempt to consolidate and survive the downturn. The resulting new company – Irish Distillers – was joined by Northern Ireland's Bushmills in 1972, and by 1976 had closed its other distilleries. By the late 1970s only two distilleries remained – Bushmills in the north and Midleton in the south, both owned by the same company.

It's here that the current era of Ireland's whiskey story begins, with the establishment of Cooley in 1987. John Teeling, an Irish entrepreneur, bought a state-owned potato vodka factory, and converted it into a whiskey

BUSHMILLS DISTILLERY. 3690. W.L.

distillery. It expanded through the 1990s, coinciding with an Irish whiskey revival in the US, driven by Irish Distillers' Jameson whiskey.

With Jameson on a world-conquering spree, Irish whiskey's poor reputation started to fall away. New whiskies from Cooley and Bushmills, as well as relaunches from the Irish Distillers back catalogue, started to appear. Pot still whiskey, produced in only small amounts since the 1950s, was revived and a host of new companies started bottling whiskey and building new distilleries.

Recent years have seen massive growth. As of 2020 there were more than 30 distilleries operational, with tens more in the planning and building stages. It's an exciting time for Irish whiskey, with new bottles hitting the shelves every day. Its growth doesn't seem to be slowing yet and, based on the great whiskeys that I've tried recently, the future is, finally, bright again.

UNITED STATES OF AMERICA

Always carry a flagon of whiskey in case of snakebite and furthermore always carry a small snake.

— W. C. Fields

THE HISTORY OF whiskey in the US is even more intertwined with the development of the country than it is in Scotland and Ireland. The country's comparatively short history means that events are much more closely documented and, while there is still a fog that hides many details, we know much more about how American whiskey came to be.

While there were some alcoholic drinks in the Americas before the arrival of Europeans, they brought both Old World tradition and distilling technology with them. Permanent camps started to spring up from the mid-1500s, and over the next century European settlers appeared along the length of the east coast.

These early settlers couldn't spare much grain for whiskey making – they needed it to eat – so while there was some distillation, much of the spirit they drank was rum, imported from the Caribbean, as well as applejack – apple brandy. However, by the time the British colonies declared independence in 1776, whiskey – or at least a spirit that was vaguely recognisable as whiskey – had become more common, using mainly rye, the most-grown grain at the time. Scottish and Irish immigrants flowed into the colonies, bringing with them not only the skills needed to make whiskey, but also a taste for the spirits of home.

Whiskey became an important trading commodity in the early days of the newly established United States, with a tax imposed on it in 1791, just eight years after the country was officially recognised by Great Britain. This was the first tax imposed by the new federal government on a domestic product, a test of its ability to enforce its will on the citizens of the new country. It was, predictably, not popular.

There followed three years of tax-dodging, a bit of civil disobedience and occasional bursts of violence. To put an end to the situation, President George Washington led an army of as many as 13,000 militia to put down a rebellious group of more than 7,000 who had gathered in western Pennsylvania to oppose the tax. The threat of force caused the rebels to disband before the militia arrived, ending the resistance without further violence. This, now known as

FAMOUS WHISKEY INS

the Whiskey Rebellion, was the new federal government's first opportunity to stand up to violent dissent, and it triumphed. While the violent side of opposition faded, political opposition continued, and the tax was repealed a few years later.

This era also saw a push west, opening up new parts of the continent for settlement. Settlers in Kentucky – which has now become the best-known whiskey-producing area – found that while rye didn't grow as well as it did out east,

ON IN PENNSYLVANIA. 1794

maize (aka corn) did. As the western borders of the US pushed further west, leading to ever more settlers going with them, corn growing increased, and distillers began to use more of the crop to make their whiskey.

It wasn't all plain sailing, though, with the temperance movement also gaining in popularity as the country grew. Father Mathew's work had crossed the Atlantic from Ireland and taken root in the religious environment of many of the states. By the 1850s, Maine and Vermont were both

WOMAN'S HOLY WAR.
Grand Charge on the Enemy's Works.

dry – alcohol was not allowed to be made or sold there – and more states followed over the subsequent years. By the start of the First World War, fourteen states were dry. Whiskey production slowed during the war, with grain redirected for food, and both during and after, more states stopped production and consumption altogether. This culminated in the National Prohibition Act, which came into effect at one minute past midnight on 17 January 1920 and forbade almost all production and sale of alcoholic drinks in the US.

The next thirteen years were ostensibly dry, but the law did not stop the people's desire for alcohol. As Scotch whisky salesman, world traveller and well-worn veteran of vice Tommy Dewar once observed, 'If you forbid a man to do a thing, you will add the joy of piracy and the zest of smuggling to his life.'

This was the era of the American gangster, now much celebrated in film and literature. Organised crime took control of the alcohol trade, ensuring distribution of illicit booze across the country in a surprisingly efficient fashion. Much of the alcohol was imported from the Caribbean and Canada, but quality was never guaranteed – it made sound financial sense to cut the real product with lower-quality spirit or other, cheaper alternatives. This led not only to people drinking poor spirits – with this era seeing the creation of many mixed drinks designed to hide the flavour of bad booze – but also drinking dangerous ones.

WHAT IS BOURBON?

In the US there are many different types of whiskey defined in law, with the most popular and well known being bourbon. While the regulations are complex, bourbon – as well as rye, wheat and corn whiskey – is defined by what it's made from.

Most American whiskey uses a mixture of different grains in its recipe. For a bourbon whiskey, this recipe must be at least 50 per cent maize; for a rye, it must be at least 50 per cent rye; and for wheat it must be at least 50 per cent wheat. The rest of the recipe is usually made up of a small amount of malted barley, with other grains used to add different flavours to the mix.

On top of the basic recipe, bourbon, rye and wheat whiskey must all be aged in new-oak casks, and there are other rules about the strength at which it can be filled into the cask, and the strength to which the whiskey can be distilled.

Just to confuse matters, corn whiskey must be at least 80 per cent maize. It also must be bottled either unaged or only after ageing in previously used casks. While the US regulations are quite straightforward, they like to throw in a few curve-balls to keep us on our toes.

By the end of the 1920s, Prohibition was increasingly unpopular, and on 5 December 1933 it was repealed. Thirteen years with little or no production in the US had left a huge hole in stocks of local whiskey, and the Scots and Canadians were ready and waiting – in some cases literally waiting on the border – to fill American liquor cabinets. Scotch and Canadian whisky flooded into the market, already well known during Prohibition, when they had been smuggled into the US. American producers started making whiskey again, but with years needed to age their spirits and the head-start that imported whisky already had, it was a hard time for them. It was the middle of the Great Depression, and it looked as if American whiskey might follow Irish whiskey into obscurity.

When the US entered the Second World War in 1941, alcohol production was diverted for military use. Imported spirits happily filled the gap, and by the end of the war, whiskey was on the ropes yet again. Rye whiskey, once the US's native spirit, almost disappeared over the following decades, relegated to a position of 'your dad's drink' as new generations of drinkers looked to vodka and unaged spirits as a way of showing how they embraced the modern world. This continued into the 1980s – the era of the vodka cocktail – but since then things have been on the up.

As the next wave of drinkers came of age, they started to look back to the drinks of their grandparents and beyond. Whiskey started to become more popular again and, with the Prohibition era glamourised on TV and in film, there began a revival of drinks from the time – both cocktails and the spirits on which they were based. While whiskey during Prohibition would have been of questionable quality, modern whiskeys are significantly better, and their popularity has continued to grow.

In the early 2000s, many states began to change their distilling regulations, making it much easier for new distillers to start making whiskey and other spirits. This led

to a boom in so-called craft distilling, with the number of distillers in the US growing from less than a hundred in 2003 to more than 2000 by 2020. While bourbon is still the US's most popular style of whiskey and more than 90 per cent is produced in Kentucky, you can now find distilleries producing whiskey of every kind all over the country.

American whiskey now encompasses both the historic brands and producers as well as new distillers, all coming together to create a huge range of styles of whiskey. With exports growing and American whiskey increasingly acclaimed, the US is claiming its spot on the world stage.

JACK DANIEL AND NATHANIEL 'NEAREST' GREEN

Jasper Newton Daniel, now known throughout the world as Jack, was born in the 1840s. For years the story of his entry into the world of distilling was that he learned from a man called Dan Call, with whom he opened the distillery that would eventually bear his name. However, more recently a different teacher has come to light – a slave by the name of Nathaniel 'Nearest' Green.

Uncle Nearest, as he was known, distilled for Call and continued to do so after he was freed. When the Jack Daniel's distillery was opened, Green continued to work with Call and Daniel, serving as its first master distiller. His descendants have continued to work at the distillery ever since.

Green's contribution was known for years, but was not part of the distillery's official history until 2017. Now, thanks to the work of author Fawn Weaver, he has been officially recognised by the distillery as its first master distiller. Weaver has also launched a foundation to honour Green's legacy, in part funded by a Tennessee whiskey that carries his name – Uncle Nearest. Ironically, it is not made by Jack Daniel's.

CANADA

The bald truth is that Canada has the money, but would rather spend it on whiskey than on books.

— Robert Barr, *Literature in Canada*

CANADA'S WHISKY HISTORY is heavily intertwined with that of Scotland, Ireland and the US, defined by European immigration and events far to its south.

While North America's earliest European settlements were in Canada thousands of years ago, the country's whisky history doesn't really begin until the late eighteenth century. Just as the newly formed US was putting down the Whiskey Rebellion, the first Canadian taxes on distilled spirits were introduced – the first documented evidence of whisky making in the country.

As elsewhere around the world, whisky making was very much a cottage industry at the time, with farmers distilling leftover grain for drinking and trade. But that quickly developed into small companies making spirit for their local areas. By the middle of the nineteenth century, Canadian whisky was being exported to the British Isles and was more popular than Scottish and Irish spirit. That didn't last long, and as Celtic whiskey began its rise, Canadian whisky disappeared in Europe and producers started to look south to the US.

This rise and fall saw the creation of whisky companies that still exist today. Rather than the Scottish and Irish, who brought distillation to Canada, commercial distilling was pioneered by English and American immigrants – Corby and Seagram were both English, and Hiram Walker was from the US.

Despite this, it was probably the Germans and the Dutch who created the modern style of Canadian whisky. Early whisky production focused on wheat, using leftovers from bread-flour making. The resulting spirit wouldn't have been the most characterful, as wheat doesn't have the punchy flavour of other grains, and when Central European immigrants suggested the addition of rye to the mix – part of their own bread-making traditions – Canadian whisky got a lot more interesting.

A little bit of rye goes a long way, packed with flavour as it is, so it's generally been used with a light touch. Despite that, Canadian whisky is commonly referred to as 'rye' across the country to this day, whether it actually contains any rye or not.

INTERIOR OF ONE OF ELEVEN MATURING WAREHOUSES.
TOTAL CAPACITY 170,000 BARRELS.

Ageing whisky has also long been part of the Canadian tradition, with laws appearing in the late nineteenth century that enforced minimums of first one and then two years in wood. Since 1974 this has been three years, aligning with regulations across Europe.

Strict rules governing whisky and a burgeoning market in the US helped Canada grow its whisky exports through the early years of the twentieth century, but it couldn't escape the world wars and the subsequent global downturn, especially as the producers were also hit by the US Prohibition – overnight, Canada's largest customer stopped buying. Well, it stopped buying legally at least, and while many distilleries closed due to Prohibition, others thrived, with the border very leaky when it came to whisky – it may have been illegal for people in the US to import whisky, but there were no laws stopping the Canadians from exporting it.

When Prohibition ended, Canadian whisky flooded into the US even more than before. This was a time in which Canadian whisky started to define itself, and began to settle on its now signature style, bringing together traditions from around the world.

Typically, Canadian whisky is made from a blend of different grains. However, rather than being combined at the beginning of production, each grain is most commonly distilled and aged separately, and blended together once mature and ready for bottling – a combination of North American ingredients and Old World techniques.

Generally, Canadian blends have been light in style, and when the US started to move away from aged spirits in the 1980s, Canadian whisky still thrived south of the border, although it was often looked down on as 'brown vodka'. With the more recent reinvigoration of the American whisky market has come growth in the number of Canadian distillers, and in experimentation. While the 1990s saw the arrival of distillers such as Forty Creek and Glenora, the 2000s have seen a boom mirroring that in the US, with craft distilleries popping up across the country. The old-fashioned distillers have not sat on their laurels, but have dug deep into their warehouses and history books, releasing experimental whiskies and reviving old names and styles long forgotten. While the newest and most experimental distillers mostly still serve local drinkers – as they did back in the earliest days of Canadian whisky making – they are slowly growing, and their whisky is starting to travel further afield. Slowly but surely, Canada is making itself known around the world again.

JAPAN

Nights without work I spend with whisky and books.

— Haruki Murakami

JAPANESE WHISKY APPEARED on the world stage relatively recently, but it has a long and vibrant history. The past couple of centuries have seen a lot of change in Japan, and whisky reflects many of the ways in which the country's society has adapted over the years.

The story traditionally starts on 8 July 1853, when American naval commodore Matthew C. Perry landed in Japan, breaking the ruling Tokugawa shogunate's policy of isolation from foreign trade. His fleet pushed past the Japanese defences into the harbour of Edo – the city now known as Tokyo – and he delivered a letter from US President Millard Fillmore demanding trading rights. He vowed to return the following year, and when he did, he not only signed the Convention of Kanagawa, opening up trade with Japan, but he also left gifts of American produce. Among those gifts was whiskey.

By the time the Tokugawa shogunate fell in 1868, foreign spirits had become well known enough to have their own word – *yoshu* – but they weren't common. The next couple of decades saw the rise of Western influence across Japan and, knowing nothing of how *yoshu* was made, producers tried to approximate it by adding flavourings to locally made spirits.

The trade deals imposed after Perry's visit were often not in Japan's favour, but the country wrested back control of imports by 1911, and in doing so it was able to add tariffs to Western spirits, finally creating a more even playing field between them and locally made *yoshu*. The industry grew over the next decade and paved the way for Japan's first native whisky distillery.

In 1917, Settsu Shuzo hired a young chemist by the name of Masataka Taketsuru. It was one of the major producers of local *yoshu*, but was looking to expand into more Western-style production methods, so Taketsuru was sent to Scotland to learn all about whisky. He spent his time working at a number of distilleries, including Longmorn, Hazelburn and Bo'ness, and returned to Japan with hands-on knowledge of whisky making and a Scottish wife – Rita. However, the company's plans had changed, and the whisky project was soon cancelled. After a couple of

years of making *yoshu* rather than the spirit he had spent his time in Scotland training to distil, he resigned and became a chemistry teacher, seemingly putting his life of whisky behind him.

A year later, in 1923, he was hired by Shinjiro Torii of Kotubukiya, a successful maker and seller of Japanese-made *yoshu* who decided that 'real' whisky was the future. His ten-year contract stated that he would make whisky for the company – finally a chance to make whisky in Japan. Torii and Taketsuru both looked for a suitable location for a distillery, and while Taketsuru favoured the more Scottish environment of the northern island of Hokkaido, Torii pushed for somewhere a bit more accessible and chose the

village of Yamazaki, between Osaka and Kyoto. The distillery was built quickly, and at 11:11 on 11 November 1924 spirit flowed at Japan's first whisky distillery.

At first it wasn't successful, with the spirit not meeting Torii's specifications, but eventually the distillery released its first product: Suntory Shirofuda – White Label. It flopped. More products followed, and the beginnings of the company that would become Japan's largest whisky producer were established. However, it was also the start of its biggest rival.

By 1930, the relationship between Yamazaki's founders had deteriorated to the extent that Taketsuru was transferred to manage a brewery in Yokohama, more than 200 miles from Osaka, keeping him away from his whisky. The brewery closed in 1933 and, with his ten-year contract up, Taketsuru left the company the next year. He had plans of his own – after a career of making whisky for someone else, it was time to do it for himself.

The founding of a company specialising in apple juice may seem like a strange turn in the story, but Taketsuru's Dai Nippon Kaju – literally 'big Japan fruit tree' – was just the beginning. While it was terrible at making juice, the company also wanted to make whisky, and built a distillery in Yoichi on Hokkaido, where Taketsuru had wanted to build a decade before.

By 1940, both Kotobukiya and Dai Nippon Kaju had successful products – Suntory Kakubin (a blended whisky still available today) and Rare Old Nikka whisky, respectively. The timing was perfect, as the start of the Second World War had stopped almost all imports. With little overseas whisky available, both companies grew during the war, despite both having production and funds redirected to the war effort.

After the war, times were incredibly hard across Japan, with widespread famine. Whisky was expensive and unobtainable by most people, although there was some demand from the occupying forces. As the years rolled on and the country recovered, however, new whisky companies sprang up and a lively bar scene – still very much part of Japanese culture today – developed. Prices fell, and whisky became

RITA TAKETSURU

While Masataka Taketsuru is often thought of as the father of Japanese whisky – he was the first distiller at Japan's first whisky distillery and the founder of its second – until recently, less was known about its mother: his wife, Jessie Roberta Taketsuru, née Cowan, better known as Rita.

In 1919, Taketsuru was studying in Glasgow and rented a room from a local family – the Cowans. He got to know the family well and proposed to one of the daughters, Rita. They married – despite opposition from both of their families – early the next year and moved back to Japan to make whisky.

Rita was a rare sight in rural Japan in the 1920s, with few foreigners living outside of the big cities, and even fewer married to a local. She weathered the storm of the Second World War, when Westerners were far from welcome in Japan, and continued to support her husband until her death in 1961. He died 18 years later, and they are buried next to each other in Yoichi, where they built their distillery.

Her story might have been forgotten if not for the Japanese television programme *Massan*. Broadcast daily in 2014 and 2015, it told a fictionalised version of her life. The adventures of Rita and Masataka – renamed Ellie and Masaharu Kameyama in the show – caught the imagination of the Japanese public, and at the programme's height one-fifth of the country were following along with their story.

the most commonly drunk spirit across the country – fresh, modern and a sign of a new Japan – supplanting *shochu*, Japan's native spirit.

By the mid-1960s, both large whisky companies were very successful and had renamed themselves after their flagship brands – Suntory and Nikka. The next decade saw a burst of building and change as other major companies entered the scene.

The 1980s were hard for whisky in Japan, with low taxation and shifts in bar culture leading to a resurgence of *shochu* drinking – paralleling the growth of vodka in the US and elsewhere. Whisky was increasingly seen as old-fashioned, switching places with *shochu* in the minds of younger drinkers. *Shochu* highballs were everywhere, and whisky consumption dropped. While there were lots of new releases in the 1980s, the local market continued to flounder and there was only one place for the whisky makers to look for growth – overseas.

Back in the 1990s and early 2000s, little Japanese whisky was exported. At the turn of the millennium, exports began to increase, thanks in part to a flurry of wins at international whisky competitions. These introduced whisky drinkers to the idea of Japanese whisky, and started to build its reputation. But as demand grew, stocks dwindled. Years of downturn in Japan had led to slower production, and the whisky makers couldn't keep up with demand. Throughout the opening decade of the new millennium, they dug ever deeper into their warehouses, but by the 2010s, supplies were running low, and favourite whiskies started to disappear and become hard to find.

The growth was a mixed blessing for the established producers, but it has ushered in a new generation of whisky. Sake, beer and *shochu* companies have turned their eyes to whisky, joined by a host of new distillers. Regulations make it difficult to start up as a whisky distillery, but there are still new producers appearing across the country every few months. Modern Japanese whisky making has begun.

KARUIZAWA

Karuizawa distillery was built in 1955 and started distilling the following year, providing the malt whisky for the Ocean range of blended whiskies. In 1976, the distiller released the first Japanese single malt, an important milestone, but as there were only a few thousand bottles available per year it wasn't well known.

Whisky's popularity peaked in Japan in the 1980s, and as it declined distillery closures were frequent. With few outlets for its whisky, a surplus of Karuizawa single malt built up in its warehouses until the distillery closed on 31 December 2000, a late victim of the downturn. It sat silent until the bulldozers rolled in and tore it down in early 2016.

This was ironic, as by the time the last brick had been taken from the site, Karuizawa whiskies had become some of the most sought after and valuable in the world.

In 2006, a Japanese/English company called Number One Drinks started bottling Karuizawa for sale overseas, buying the casks that were still sat in the distillery's warehouses. They were hugely popular – often compared to some of the finest old-school Scotch whiskies – and by the time the distillery was demolished, bottles were appearing at auction for tens of thousands of pounds.

Sadly, Karuizawa's malt has become a whisky that is now collected rather than drunk. It is a distillery that has been lost twice – first when it closed, and a second time now that its whisky is rarely opened and enjoyed.

Japanese Single Malt Whisky

KARUIZAWA SINGLE MALT WHISKY
Specially selected by La Maison du Whisky

DISTILLED IN
1984
BOTTLED IN
2012
CASK #7975
DISTILLED, MATURED
& BOTTLED IN JAPAN

70cl

PRODUCT OF JAPAN
DISTILLED, MATURED & BOTTLED IN JAPAN
IMPORTED BY LA MAISON DU WHISKY
8/10 RUE GUSTAVE EIFFEL, 92110 CLICHY, FRANCE

59.3%

THE REST OF THE WORLD

*Whisky now belongs not to the Scots but to the world
at large.*

— Aeneas Macdonald, *Scotch*

WHISKY IS NOW truly a worldwide drink. As bottles have
made their way around the globe, fans have turned their
eyes towards making their own. Pretty much every country
in the world now has someone making whisky, from small
countries like Singapore to places such as Pakistan that you
might not expect.

We start with the world's largest whisky market: India.
That title is often disputed, as India's definition of whisky
doesn't quite match up with that of the rest of the world – it
is often a mix of spirits that aren't necessarily made from
grain. While this mostly means that Indian 'whisky' is rarely
seen outside of India, a few producers make spirit that the
rest of the world sees as whisky, and increasingly these have
been turning heads.

The first to hit the market was Amrut, which launched its single malt in maybe the most difficult whisky market in the world: Glasgow, Scotland. Its origin hidden in blind tastings, it slowly picked up fans and has now spread not only across Scotland and the UK, but also Europe, Asia and the US, picking up awards as it has gone. More distillers have since followed, and Indian whisky has gone from being unknown to respected in an astonishingly short space of time.

When it comes to impressive rises, Taiwan is the poster child for international whisky success. Long a huge importer of whisky, the country didn't make any of its own until after it joined the World Trade Organization in 2002 – when regulations changed and local whisky making became much more viable. In 2005, King Car Group, a company whose business spans from canned coffee to biotech, built a distillery in the northeast of Taiwan – Kavalan. Since then, it has rapidly grown to become a powerhouse in Asia and one of the world's most feted whisky producers.

Heading south, we come to Australia, which has been a part of the whisky world for almost as long as the US and Canada. After Europeans arrived, whisky production started pretty quickly, although the country's early years as a penal colony meant that it was almost all illicit. Since then, Australia has undergone various booms and busts, not really making a name for itself on the world stage until relatively recently.

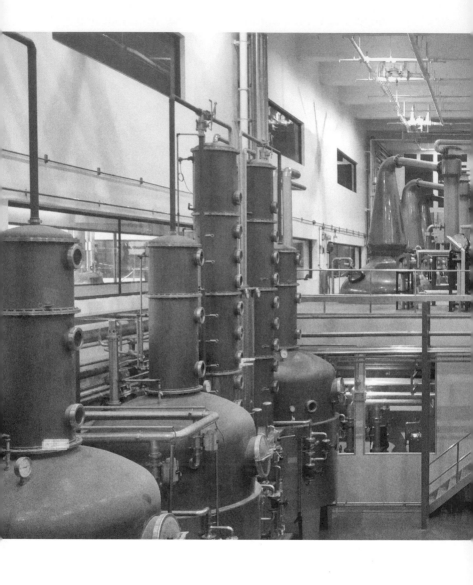

In the 1990s, the Lark family managed to get a distillation licence and started producing whisky in Tasmania. Since then, the number of distilleries has grown to more than twenty on the island, and hundreds more have opened across the country. As with Australia's growth to becoming one of the world's top wine producers, its whisky is building a formidable reputation while creating its own distinctive styles.

Heading west, we eventually arrive at Africa. While there has been some whisky making across the wider continent, it's South Africa where it has really taken root. The James Sedgwick Distillery near Cape Town has been at the heart of it, with its Three Ships single malt and Bain's Cape Mountain single grain firmly placing the country on the whisky-making map.

Looking north, we have Europe, an area familiar with distillation for centuries. Beyond whisky, there are a huge number of local distillation traditions, from the grape brandies of Cognac and Armagnac, and the fruity palinkas of Hungary and its neighbours, to the vodkas of Eastern and Northern Europe, and the herbal spirits of the mountains and south. With the rise of whisky around the world, many distillers have turned their attention to grain and combined their traditional processes with whisky making, with various degrees of success. While you can now readily find French, German, Spanish, Italian and Dutch whisky, with distilleries in Poland, Croatia and the Czech Republic among others also in full swing, the Nordic countries have become the best-known new European whisky makers.

Things started with Mackmyra in Sweden, the first Nordic distillery to release single malt whisky, but since then whisky making has expanded across the region. There are distilleries in Denmark, a few dotted around Finland, one north of the Arctic Circle in Norway, one in Iceland that dries its malt using sheep dung and even a project to open a distillery in the Faroe Islands. Long known for being the home of some of Europe's hardest drinkers and most ardent whisky lovers, the Nordics are now also host to some of the continent's most exciting distillers.

Hopping back over the North Sea, we return to the UK. While there were distillers making whisky in England and Wales for centuries, that all died out in the early twentieth century. However, the twenty-first has seen a revival, with new distilleries popping up across both.

Wales is quieter than its neighbour, with Penderyn the first new distillery in almost a century when it opened in 2004. More are now appearing, but there's much more happening over the border in England.

The Nelstrop family are Norfolk grain farmers who have been sending much of their barley north to Scotland to make whisky for years. Head of the family James Nelstrop was thinking of retiring – and, looking for a project to keep him occupied, thought that setting up a small whisky distillery would do the trick. Working with son Andrew, he quickly realised that the law restricted the size of distilleries and that building a small one wasn't allowed. Plans changed and expanded, and England's first distillery in more than a century opened near Norwich in 2006 – St George's Distillery, home of The English Whisky Company.

The licensing laws that forced The English Whisky Company into expanding its plans have since been tweaked, allowing smaller distillers to build distilleries and leading to a boom in British craft distilling. England has new distillers appearing regularly, with whisky already on the shelves from many of them, and much more on the way.

It doesn't stop there. If there's grain, water, wood and people who like whisky, then there is invariably someone making whisky. South and Central America drink a lot of whisky made overseas, but with Argentinian whisky already on the market, Mexico making early forays and other projects starting up, we will soon see more. While I don't expect to see an official Antarctic distillery emerging any time soon – although if at least one of the bases doesn't have an illicit still, I feel we have failed as a species – the gaps in the whisky-making world are filling in. Soon you'll be able to grab locally made whisky no matter where you are

DRINKING WHISKY

The water was not fit to drink. To make it palatable, we had to add whisky. By diligent effort, I learned to like it.

— Winston Churchill

DRINKING WHISKY IS really simple – you pour it into the largest of the various holes in your face. Whisky fans often talk about taking their time over a dram, focusing their attention solely on the whisky. To be honest, that's not how I drink whisky most of the time – ignoring your drinking companions while you sit silently and contemplate your glass is a surefire way to have no one to go to the pub with. However, if you want to get the most out of your drink, you can take things a little further than necking shots of whisky and focus more on tasting it.

Flavour is complex, and how we discern it is even more so. Tasting a whisky is a multi-faceted experience which involves all five of our senses.

"They always serve the finest drinks"

BOTTLED IN BOND

OLD FORESTER

KENTUCKY STRAIGHT BOURBON WHISKY

AS IT SAYS ON THE LABEL: *"There is nothing better in the market"*

To honor the guest whose friendship you cherish, always serve *America's Guest Whisky*,
famous bonded Old Forester. As fine in quality, as elegant in flavor as it was in 1870—
the year the first Old Forester was created to set a standard for all Kentucky whiskies.

KENTUCKY STRAIGHT BOURBON WHISKY • BOTTLED IN BOND • 100 PROOF

BROWN-FORMAN DISTILLERS CORPORATION • AT LOUISVILLE IN KENTUCKY

☞ HEARING: The pop of a cork, the scrape of a cap, the glug of whisky being poured into a glass – these are all important parts of tasting. They set the scene and get your brain prepared for what comes next.

☞ SIGHT: How does the whisky look in the glass? How does it move when you swirl it? Does it stick to the glass and run slowly down the sides in sensuous tears? How does the colour change as you move it around? Does it look appealing? While you can't tell much about how good a whisky is from how it looks, you can make some good guesses about how it might feel in the mouth.

☞ SMELL: What can you smell? What does it remind you of? People, places, objects, food, drink? Smell is the most important part of experiencing a whisky, so take your time.

☞ TASTE: Your tongue doesn't operate in isolation, and you have taste buds all over your mouth. Roll the whisky around, and make sure it touches every part of your palate.

☞ TOUCH: Your mouth doesn't only taste, it also feels. As you move the whisky around your mouth, what does it feel like? Does it have a silky texture, or is it spiky? Is it rich and oily or thin and watery?

While smell and taste will dominate your impressions of a whisky, the other senses are key to the overall experience – tasting whisky is much more than just a scientific analysis. Smell and taste are closely linked: your nose is a sensitive organ and can pick up much more nuance than your mouth, which will detect broader swathes of flavour – salty, sour, sweet, bitter and savoury (also known as *umami*). However, it's when nose and mouth combine that you get the full measure of a whisky. Your nose and mouth are connected at the back of the palate. When you eat or drink something, the aroma will travel into the back of your nose from your mouth, and you will smell it as well as taste it. It's this combination that gives the complexity of flavour that we find in food and drink, and the reason why you can't taste much when you hold your nose.

Here's my five-step approach to tasting whisky. This is just a starting point, and should be adapted, tweaked and ignored as much as you like – tasting whisky is all about getting the most out of your glass, and everyone is different.

1. Look at your whisky. Hold it up to the light. Enjoy its colour.
2. Smell your whisky. Don't jam your nose into the glass, but move it slowly towards you, sniffing along the way. Switch nostrils. Move it around. You'll find a host of different aromas as you do.

3. Take a little sip of the whisky and swallow it without thinking too much – this primes your mouth and gets it ready for a proper taste.
4. Take a larger sip and roll it around the mouth – make sure it hits as many taste buds as possible. Once you've had enough of that, swallow your whisky.
5. Now think about what lingers – the aftertaste or 'finish'. How long does it last? Does it change? Is it simple or complex?

With a little extra contemplation, you can unlock new layers of flavour in your whisky and get much more out of it than by knocking it back without a thought.

Once you've started tasting whisky, it's time to think about glasses. The shape of your glass will impact how you experience any drink, changing how it smells and tastes. A standard tumbler is a great all-round glass, easy to drink out of and fairly neutral when it comes to amplifying or hiding aroma and taste. Meanwhile a specialised tasting glass, with a rounded bowl and a tapered mouth, will concentrate aroma and direct the drink to the centre of your tongue, giving it more intensity.

Glasses are very personal things, and different ones are great for different occasions – hanging out with friends is very different from judging a whisky competition. As with tasting, experiment and find out what works best for you. And try not to buy too many – a whisky glassware obsession can quickly overwhelm the amount of cupboard space you have …

While tasting a whisky on its own is often seen as the purest way to enjoy it, it's far from the only way – whisky is just an ingredient, in the end, and manipulating it to increase your enjoyment of it is no bad thing.

The first way to change how a whisky tastes easily is by altering its temperature. As you change the temperature, different flavour compounds will become more or less detectable, and not in a simple fashion – when cold, a whisky will have less aroma, but some specific aromas that are more difficult to detect when warm will be much more obvious. Along with the change in flavour, you will also find that the texture changes with temperature, making things even more complicated. If you want to experiment, put some whisky in the fridge and some more by the stove, and then try them alongside some that's just been pulled out of your drinks cabinet – you'll find them all quite different, even though they're the same whisky.

Along with changing the temperature comes one of the most-discussed considerations in the whisky world – the addition of water and ice. Water and ice will dilute your whisky, which will both reduce the concentration of alcohol and change the way that it tastes – and just like when we change the temperature, the way the flavours change

with dilution is complicated. You don't need to add much water – even a few drops will change things, breaking the surface tension of your whisky and releasing aromas as well as increasing the dilution. Add in the cooling effect of ice and we've now got even more variables changing at the same time – it's hard to predict what a whisky will taste like after you've popped in a cube or two. Again, it's time for experimentation: add some ice to your whisky and try it alongside some straight from the bottle.

The next step is to add something more to your whisky. The simplest addition is more water. In Japan it is very common to mix whisky with still water and ice – a style known as *mizuwari*, or 'diluted with water' – to make a long drink. Whisky and soda water, now better known as a whisky highball, has also long been a favourite. The gentle sourness of the soda water adds another layer of flavour at the same time as its fizz brings a different texture to the mix. Keeping things simple, we can switch out water for a different, more flavoursome mixer – this is how most whisky is drunk around the world. While the most common 'whisky and …' combo is probably Coke (other colas are available), it's far from the only one. Sparkling citrus drinks and ginger ale are common in the West. In the East, we find green tea as a popular addition, with blended Scotch whisky and tea a mainstay of bars in Hong Kong. Different combinations of soft drink and whisky can create wildly varied flavour combinations, and finding a favourite can take lots of experimentation. For example, American whiskeys can work very well with cloudy lemonade, their punchy sweetness working well against the zing of the citrus, and smoky whiskies go very well with Coke – it might be sacrilege to fans of peaty Scotch, but after a couple of Smoky Cokies it's hard to deny.

Taking things further, we move on to cocktails. Again, while this might seem heretical to some, whisky is a flavoursome ingredient as well as a drink to be enjoyed on its own. As long as you choose an appropriate whisky that will complement the other ingredients you are using, whisky cocktails can be excellent. Here are a few classics to get you going, but don't be afraid to experiment with the recipes.

THE OLD FASHIONED

As the name suggests, this cocktail has been around for a while. It's pretty much the simplest drink you can make that steps beyond a 'Whisky and …', but it can be made very different with tiny tweaks to your ingredients and method. Here's the simplest way of making one, but you should definitely experiment with the ratios, the amount of stirring, the type of sweetener you use … everything.

60 ml whisky (usually American whiskey)
1 sugar cube
Angostura bitters

Put your sugar cube in a glass and soak it with Angostura bitters – two or three dashes should do it. Give it a few seconds to loosen up and then squish it into a paste. Add a little splash of whisky and mix until dissolved. Add some ice and half the whisky, and give things a stir. Once you are bored of stirring, add the rest of the whisky and some more ice, and keep stirring. Again, once boredom sets in and you feel you really need a drink, stop stirring and have a taste.

VARIATION: Use Peychaud's bitters instead of Angostura and strain the drink into a new glass that you have rinsed with a little bit of absinthe. You now have a Sazerac.

THE MANHATTAN

The Martini of American whiskey cocktails, this is one of the most classic of all pre-Prohibition drinks. Manhattans are one of the reasons why my fridge always has a bottle of sweet vermouth in the door.

50 ml American whiskey (rye whiskey is traditional)
20 ml sweet vermouth
Angostura bitters

Add the whisky and vermouth to a stirring glass with a dash of bitters. Add ice, stir until very cold and strain into a glass. Garnish with a cocktail cherry.

VARIATION: Use Scotch whisky instead of American to make a Rob Roy.

MANHATTAN COCKTAIL
1 part Italian Vermouth
3 parts Spring Garden Rye
Shake, strain and add Cherry

Manhattan Cocktail

At the fashionable places today, the Manhattan cocktail is again the correct aperitif, just as it was in the days of Martin's, Sherry's and the old Beaux Arts when it was made with authentic Spring Garden Rye. Aging for you through all the slow years in charred white oak barrels, this fine whiskey now comes to you in a mellow blend which has taken on added character and distinction.

PENN-MARYLAND COMPANY, INC.
52 William St., New York

Rye

Back through the generations, the name of SPRING GARDEN has been known and highly cherished among Rye whiskies. And now its fine flavor and quality come to you in a rich blend eminently worth its price

"Mine Host's Handbook," 32 pages of information about the use, traditions, and service of fine spirits, with time-honored recipes. Send 10c to Room 1225, Penn-Maryland Company, Inc., 52 William Street, New York

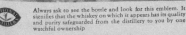

Always ask to see the bottle and look for this emblem. It signifies that the whiskey on which it appears has its quality and purity safeguarded from the distillery to you by one watchful ownership

This advertisement is not intended to offer alcoholic beverages for sale or delivery in any state or community wherein the sale or use thereof is unlawful

WHISKY SOUR

This is the drink that made me realise that American whiskey in a cocktail can be a good thing – and it's one of the reasons why I get quite so much vitamin C in my diet.

    50 ml whisky (usually American whiskey)
    30 ml fresh lemon juice (don't use bottled stuff,
        it's nasty)
    10 ml sugar syrup
    Egg white (optional, but it gives a beautiful foam on
        the drink)

If using an egg, first shake the ingredients together without ice until foamy, then add ice and shake again until chilled. Otherwise, just shake with ice. Strain into a glass filled with ice and garnish with a cherry.

VARIATION: This is a traditional, spirit-forward version, but it's very much a drink of personal taste – I often go with double the amount of juice and sugar, to make a much longer drink.

IRISH COFFEE

The perfect after dinner drink (or before dinner, or at lunchtime, or whenever really), this is often made fairly badly, with just a splash of Irish whiskey added to a cup of coffee. To do it right, you need a bit of creamy decadence.

25 ml Irish whiskey
100 ml black coffee (freshly brewed and hot)
25 ml lightly whipped cream
Brown sugar

Stir the sugar into the coffee while still hot, and let it cool to a little warmer than drinking temperature. Add the whiskey and pour into a glass with a handle – picking up a tumbler of hot coffee is a surefire way to lose your fingerprints. Carefully layer the cream on top, so that it settles in a flat layer. Drink the coffee through the cream.

PENICILLIN

Most whisky cocktails are classics from Prohibition and before that, and use American spirit, but the Penicillin is a modern drink that focuses on the flavour of Scotch whisky. It was first served at legendary bar Milk & Honey in New York in 2005, and has quickly become a classic in its own right. It's an updated version of a traditional cure-all: whisky and lemon – it might not have the effectiveness of actual penicillin, but it can certainly make you feel better.

One ingredient needs a little bit of work – honey syrup: combine equal parts of honey and water in a pan, and heat until combined.

50 ml non-smoky Scotch whisky
20 ml fresh lemon juice
20 ml honey syrup
5 ml smoky Scotch whisky
2 slices of fresh ginger

Smash up the ginger in the bottom of a shaker and then add the non-smoky whisky, juice and syrup. Shake with ice and strain into a chilled glass. Gently float the smoky whisky on top of the cocktail and garnish with candied ginger.

THE SOURTOE COCKTAIL

There are hundreds of whisky cocktails made around the world, but the strangest of all may well be the Sourtoe, only found at the Sourdough Hotel in Dawson, Yukon.

It's not strictly a cocktail, and the recipe has changed over the years, with only a single ingredient remaining the same: a preserved human toe.

Simply put, it's any drink on the bar's menu – traditionally a shot of whisky – with the toe in it. The story goes that the first toe belonged to a miner, who kept it in a jar of alcohol after it was amputated due to frostbite. A local found the jar after the miner died, took it down to his local saloon and started dropping the toe in people's drinks for fun. Over the years the toe has been replaced with new donations after previous ones have been lost, stolen and swallowed, but people now ask for the toe.

If you swallow it, you have to pay a fine, but otherwise there is only one rule for consuming the drink: you can drink it fast, you can drink it slow – but the lips have gotta touch the toe.

There are strong opinions among whisky fans about how whisky should be drunk, but in the end the answer is very simple: you should drink your whisky however you want. Be open to experimentation and don't discount things until you've tried them – but, most of all, don't tell anyone else how to drink theirs.

THE FUTURE OF WHISKY

*A good gulp of hot whisky at bedtime – it's not very
scientific, but it helps.*

— Alexander Fleming

IT IS A VERY exciting time for whisky. There's never been so
much of it and its popularity continues to rise, with people
around the world not only drinking whisky but also making
it. The Old World's monopoly on brown grain spirit has
very much been broken, and new styles are popping up all
the time, expanding the definition of whisky and introduc-
ing new people to the ever-increasing worldwide whisky
community.

With that increasing popularity comes change. Changes
to who is drinking, changes to who is buying and changes to
how whisky is made. The more conservative end of whisky
fandom may grumble, but it's an inevitable process we have
seen happen continuously over the centuries, and it's one
that isn't going to slow down or stop.

First, the people who drink whisky have changed a lot over the years as society's attitudes have changed. In these more egalitarian times, whisky is very much the drink of the people, a status it has dipped into repeatedly throughout its history. More recently seen as an 'old man's drink', the gradual change in attitudes towards food and drink is opening whisky up to everyone and pushing beyond the more closed-minded expectations of style to create new and interesting drinks. The change is slow, but as society continues to remodel itself, so whisky follows.

The drink's booming popularity has also created a new market – investment whisky. While there has long been a secondary market for whisky, with long sold-out bottles appearing at auction and making tidy sums for their owners, the current situation is causing alarm among long-time drinkers. Often, whiskies appear that don't seem to be designed to be drunk, with fancy boxes and bottles, increasingly complex stories of creation and eye-watering price tags putting them outside both the interest and the budget of the everyday drinker. Along with those, bottles from the past with fearsome reputations are also commanding premiums, with some fetching hundreds of thousands of pounds at auction, and a few already pipping the million mark. Some of these bottles are opened and drunk (no matter how much you are willing to spend on a bottle to drink, there are always people who are very happy to spend more, as well as those who think the amount you are spending is ridiculous), but they are also collected like art, cars, watches or a whole host of other luxury items. Investors with little interest in whisky are now joining the fray along with investment companies, happy to help anyone with some spare money buy into whisky as the latest alternative investment. As with any investing, there is an element of gambling, and no doubt people will make small fortunes, but we should never forget the ever-present warning: 'The value of your investment can go down as well as up.'

With the market growing and more people wanting whisky – whether for drinking or other reasons – research has continued into ways of making whisky more efficiently and for less money. This has been going on throughout whisky's history, with everything from the types of grain used to the technology in distilleries changing to give whisky makers the tools to do things faster and cheaper. This is rapidly approaching an end game, with labs pushing the boundaries towards a production singularity – put ingredients in one end of the machine, press a button, wait a bit, collect whisky from the other end.

It is still early days, but with each project that builds a reactor to attempt to emulate years of ageing in months, days and weeks, we move nearer to a future where whisky can be dialled up on demand. The artificially aged whisky isn't up to the standards of traditionally made whisky yet, but every day it takes a step closer in quality, with spirits that are in some cases attempted copies but in others are new in style and character, further expanding what we might think of as whisky. Taking that idea to the absolute limit, we also find companies combining pure flavour compounds with alcohol to create whisky-flavoured spirits – no maturation, no magic machines, just a bucket, some bottles and a stirring stick. As with artificially aged spirit, they're definitely not up with 'real' whisky yet, but they too are getting better all the time.

This brings us back to a hard question, and one that, despite pages of words, this book hasn't answered – what is whisky? Is it the end product? Is it the taste? Is it how it's made? Is it the people who made it? Whisky is something different to everyone, and what you get from one might be entirely different from what I do. Whether we like the flavours, have visited the distillery, know the makers, like the bottle, appreciate its colour or like the ethos of how it is made – there are many factors that will affect our enjoyment of a glass of whisky. Despite all of that, there is thankfully one aspect whose importance we can agree on, even if we may not agree when swapping whisky stories:

Does it taste nice?

FURTHER READING

Whisk(e)y
Dave Broom, *The World Atlas of Whisky* (Mitchell Beazley, 2014)
Eddie Ludlow, *Whisky: A Tasting Course* (DK, 2019)
Ingvar Ronde, *The Malt Whisky Year Book* (MagDig Media, 2020)
Dave Waddell, *The Knowledge: Whisky* (Quadrille, 2015)

American Whiskey
Fred Minnick, *Bourbon: The Rise, Fall and Rebirth of an American Whiskey* (Voyageur Press, 2016)
Michael R. Veach, *Kentucky Bourbon Whiskey* (University Press of Kentucky, 2013)

Canadian Whisky
Davin de Kergommeaux, *Canadian Whisky* (McClelland & Stewart, 2014)

Irish Whiskey
Peter Mulryan, *The Whiskeys of Ireland* (O'Brien Press, 2016)

Fionnan O'Connor, *A Glass Apart* (Images Publishing Group, 2017)

Japanese Whisky

Dominic Roskrow, *Whisky Japan* (Kodansha, 2016)

Stefan Van Eycken, *Whisky Rising* (Cider Mills Press, 2017)

Scotch Whisky

Emmanuel Dron, *Collecting Scotch Whisky: An Illustrated Encyclopedia, vol. 1: 19th & 20th Century* (self-published, 2017)

Michael Jackson, *Malt Whisky Companion* (DK, 2010)

Andrew Jefford, *Peat Smoke and Spirit* (Headline, 2004)

Flavour and Aroma

Harold McGee, *Nose Dive* (John Murray, 2020)

Charles Spence, *Gastrophysics* (Penguin, 2017)

LIST OF ILLUSTRATIONS

Also available in this series

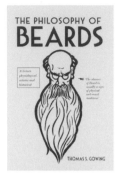

THE PHILOSOPHY OF BEARDS

THOMAS S. GOWING

THE PHILOSOPHY OF COFFEE

BRIAN WILLIAMS

THE PHILOSOPHY OF WINE

RUTH BALL

THE PHILOSOPHY OF TEA

TONY GEBELY

THE PHILOSOPHY OF GIN

JANE PEYTON

THE PHILOSOPHY OF CHEESE

PATRICK McGUIGAN

THE PHILOSOPHY OF BEER

JANE PEYTON

THE PHILOSOPHY OF TATTOOS

JOHN MILLER